Ana Claudia Piovesan

Definition of profiles and roles:

Ana Claudia Piovesan

Definition of profiles and roles:

Improving processes from the organisation of Human Resources

ScienciaScripts

Imprint

Cover image: www.ingimage.com

This book is a translation from the original published under ISBN 978-613-9-70501-6.

Publisher:
Sciencia Scripts
is a trademark of
Dodo Books Indian Ocean Ltd. and OmniScriptum S.R.L publishing group

120 High Road, East Finchley, London, N2 9ED, United Kingdom
Str. Armeneasca 28/1, office 1, Chisinau MD-2012, Republic of Moldova, Europe
Printed at: see last page
ISBN: 978-620-7-84720-4

SUMMARY

This article presents the organization of guidelines for human resources in project management, presenting the possible profiles and roles within an IT organization. For organizations aiming to improve their project management processes, it is necessary to align tasks within these processes with a team that has the skills and profile for this activity. The main objective of this work was to present the results of defining roles by competencies to take on project activities, which contributes to people management and also the types of profiles that leaders need to have for each type of role. What's more, once you know what each employee's position and skills are, it's even easier to remunerate these members of the company. The methodology used is a case study that follows the definition of the roles and competencies required for positions within software development projects. The work aimed to cover an area that is little researched and carried out in projects linked to IT companies, since it is a very important role for people management within any organization.

Keywords: Profiles. Roles. Skills. Software development.

SUMMARY

1 INTRODUCTION

Organizations are racing to define roles in order to better delegate activities to professionals who really have the skills needed to carry out that activity. Currently, the big problem for organizations is being able to define their profiles and roles within their production process, leading them to hire professionals who are not really what the company needs to carry out that particular activity. With the competencies of each professional well aligned with the activities they will perform, it is very easy for the organization to increase productivity and seek to reward those professionals who do what they are supposed to (ROBBINS, 2000).

The main objective of this work is to describe each position and role within an organization, to make it easier to delimit the tasks that the company carries out and also to make it easier to manage people, thus helping the leadership to have more knowledge of what each employee is responsible for within the company. Before drawing up these role definitions, the company did not have an alignment of what activities an employee should carry out and what the competencies of each one of them should be for the function hired. For this reason, all the positions and roles within the company were reformulated, seeking to analyze what was done in other large companies.

This work deals with the definition of profiles and roles within an IT organization, since it is very difficult for organizations to match these positions with the competencies of each one, and since technology companies need to follow a maturity model for the development of their products, it becomes much more difficult to align the human resources team with the software development process through a maturity model for the software development process.

This article has the following section structure, in addition to this introduction: Basis, methodology and results of the elaboration of positions and functions for each of the company's sectors, including product development, support, implementation and the product sales sector.

2 THEORETICAL BASIS

This section will present concepts related to the importance of the human being for organizations, with the definition of roles, alignment between human resources and organizational strategy, people management, knowledge and other concepts.

2.1 IMPORTANCE OF THE HUMAN BEING

Human beings appeared on earth to make sense of things, because at the beginning of life on earth there were only animals and plants, soon after which human beings discovered fire and thus began to make sense of the other things that were already part of the earth. Many of these human beings began to carry out research and experiments to find out what they could do to improve their lives or even to cure certain diseases (COSTA, 2016).

After many decades of research and experimentation, thousands of things have been discovered that could be done through innovation, creativity and human intelligence. In this sense, most technological innovations are due to the ability of human beings to have new ways of seeing the world, seeking to improve tasks in different sectors (TOMAEL, M. I; ALCARA, A. R.; CHIARA, I. G., 2005).

In this way, we can see that human beings, in addition to building and transforming the world around them, also transform and build themselves through the experiences and relationships they establish throughout their lives, which is why organizations always need to keep their human capital motivated. According to Fleury (2002), a process of change is the result of previous practices or experiences, which may or may not manifest itself in a perceptible change in behavior.

According to Chiavenato (2012), this century saw three organizational eras:

- The era of classic industrialization - refers to the period after the Industrial Revolution, up to the mid-1950s and half of the 20th century. The organizational culture was focused on the past and on valuing and preserving traditions. People were considered production resources. At this time, industrial relations departments and personnel departments emerged, designed to make employees comply with organizational requirements and standards. Employees were seen only as providers of physical and muscular effort, where a large workforce predominated.
- Neoclassical era: the period from the 1950s to the 1990s, right after the Second World War. Classical theory was replaced by neoclassical management theory. The bureaucratic model was resized by structuralist theory and human relations theory was replaced by behavioral theory.
- The Information Age: from 1990 to the present day. It was the era of rapid and unexpected change. It has developed greatly and has come to influence the behavior of organizations in relation to people. Modern organizations have left behind the classical and neoclassical era of management, of valuing old traditions and changing the way they think, act and manage people. As a result, the personnel department is now called the human resources department.

The main objective of apprenticeships is to seek innovation in various areas of activity, in which people continually improve their skills by working together on research or more complex issues, providing personal changes so that other people can develop these new skills and competitiveness in the future (TOMAEL, M. I; ALCARA, A. R.; CHIARA, I. G., 2005, p.99).

With the evolution of human beings, we have many inventions that help us in our day-to-day activities, such as the internet, computers, cell phones, social networks, vehicles, houses, buildings and other things that we can enjoy comfortably. In this sense, people have come to care more about material goods than about their own essence, and their main values and experiences over time (ROBBINS, 2000).

Nowadays, due to the constant economic, technological and social changes, it is of fundamental importance for organizations to focus on human resource management and it is becoming clear that the competitive edge of organizations lies in the people they employ and their available resources.

2.1.1 The importance of human beings in organizations

Companies are increasingly valuing their employees, recognizing that it is through them that improvements are made within organizations. One way of finding out if a company has good employees is through the products it produces, because it is from these that we can see how much the employee dedicates themselves and applies their admiration to what they build (CHIAVENATO, 2010).

Companies are always made up of people, regardless of their physical or technological structure, since it is people who are responsible for managing the entire structure. According to Chiavenato (2010, p.5), "without organizations and people, there would be no People Management", because organizations are made up of people and organizations depend on them to achieve their objectives and fulfil their missions.

For companies to act strategically, they need to consider people as relevant and fundamental tools, as they are responsible for generating a promising and successful future for the company. Bearing in mind that human behavior is a differentiating element for adding value to companies and becomes a sustained competitive advantage, as it helps to meet the challenges of business competitiveness (FISCHER, 2000).

The main asset of organizations is the human being, and their motivation must be constant. The roles of each professional and who carries them out must be well defined. It is necessary to understand how to administer, and to manage effectively, and administering, according to Lacombe (2006), means having a set of efforts aimed at planning, organizing, directing or leading, coordinating and controlling the activities of a group of people who have common objectives.

Another asset of an organization is undoubtedly its workforce. Good people management is necessary to ensure that employees are willing to work for the company in order to achieve its objectives. On the other hand, employees expect to receive salaries that are fair to their role and benefits that enable them to perform their established tasks better and better (DUTRA, 2002).

2.1.2 Alignment between human resources and organizational strategy

From a business perspective, the concept of a people management model is important because it seeks to identify patterns of behavior aligned with the company's business. For Dutra (2002), this comes from the fact that changes in organizations are not limited to organizational structures, products or markets, "but to behavioural, cultural, political and internal power relations patterns" (DUTRA, 2002, p.37), constantly evolving in companies.

Among the competitive advantages raised by organizations, one that is closer to the interests of this work is the competitive advantage of having special talents in the company (LACOMBE, 2006). However, this was not always the case, because at the height of strategic planning, it was the determination of the risks that a company was running by the knowledge and competence of its top managers and their vocation for business.

In the quest for organizations to have competitive advantages to maintain their survival, the modernization of strategies has made it the responsibility of the operational, middle and lower levels of management, where the advantages are actually achieved. The need to expand internal skills is a fundamental point for improving the qualification and specialization of employees, and awareness and preparation must come from HR (Human

Resources) professionals for this highly strategic role, which is essential for their survival (ULRICH, 2003).

An organization needs to follow ethical standards and social responsibility, and every organization needs to give importance to this issue, as this would reduce many of the problems, as well as maintaining a fairer and better environment, one of appreciation and respect. In addition, HR Management seeks to manage and drive change, which is always welcome and extremely important so that the organization can always seek improvement and better quality, as well as better results in different sectors (ULRICH, 2003).

One aspect of organizational strategies is their alignment with the people management function. Strategic HR planning refers to the way in which the HR function can contribute to the achievement of organizational objectives and, at the same time, favour and encourage the achievement of individual employee objectives (WREN, 2005).

Planning is based on a philosophy of action and is described in three types:

- Conservative planning: planning more geared towards stability and maintaining the existing situation. Decisions are made in order to obtain good results, but it is unlikely that this planning will seek to make radical changes to the organization.
- Optimizing planning: more focused on the organization's adaptability and innovation. Decisions are made to obtain the best possible results by minimizing resources or maximizing performance in order to make the best use of available resources.
- Foresight planning: planning for contingencies and the future of the organization. Decisions are made in order to reconcile the different interests involved, through a composition capable of leading to results for the natural development of the company and adjusting them to the contingencies that arise along the way.

Strategic people management planning can be drawn up and designed after the company's strategic planning. In order to achieve their full potential, organizations need to have the right people available to do the job.

2.1.3 Agent of transformation and change

The so-called operational functions, such as administering infrastructure and managing employee contributions, are complemented by the strategic functions, where they help to define new business strategies, thus generating transformations and changes (ULRICH, 2000). Over the years, organizations have become increasingly aware of the need to adopt corporate governance principles, which determine the main decisions that will be made based on the objectives and preservation of the business.

The HR area has become increasingly present as a negotiating agent in various sectors of the workplace. However, they are often not present in all segments and focus on companies with strong brands, together with consumers or the community, with high technological innovation or with differentiated products on the market (FISCHER, 2000). Their roles are preponderant, both operational and strategic, and must be considered in order to achieve good results for the companies and the people who work in them, distinguishing themselves from the others and making them more competitive through their skills and specializations (ULRICH, 2000).

In the 1970s, the concept of human resource management began to emerge, but it still had a lot of problems because it had not managed to completely change the ideas of the people who make up organizations, but even so, workers are only seen as productive resources (CHIAVENATO, 2008).

In this way, the Human Resources area becomes essential in an organization, and Chiavenato (2010, p. 15) argues that it is becoming increasingly complex and challenging in every way, including training and even the emotional part of people. To confirm the fact that Human Resources

Management is essential, Gil (2007, p. 15) states that "the end of Human Resources Management can only occur after the end of all the other areas of Management, because all the other resources of organizations are managed by their human resources".

Another important objective within an organization is to follow ethical standards and social responsibility, pointing out that the whole organization should be concerned about this, as this would certainly reduce problems, generating a fairer and better environment, one of appreciation and respect. In addition, HR Management seeks to manage and drive change, which is always welcome and extremely important so that the organization can always seek improvement and better quality, as well as better results (ROBBINS, 2000).

2.1.4 People management factors

The factors of people management will present the performance within an organization, and a management model that can be followed by it, in which they are divided into internal and external factors (ALBUQUERQUE *et al.* 2009):

Internal factors:

- Technology adopted: the employee's performance will depend on the context and especially the pace of the machines and the technology adopted.
- Work Organization Strategy: this factor aims to find the behavior required by the job, for example, a machine operator must work according to the job, and in order for him to work in a certain way, we have the work organization strategy.
- Organizational culture: it is evident that every organization has its own organizational culture, and it is very visible in our daily lives. As an example, we have software engineers who are more valued than developers, increasingly characterizing different organizational cultures.
- Organizational Structure: this is considered a very important internal factor

within the organization, as it represents details of fundamental importance for good performance and use of resources. The structure can thus have two distinct types, the departmental, which implies an equally segmented and restricted model, and the matrix, by business or networks.

External factors:

External factors are considered to be another very important point for the organization, in which the competencies and organizational profiles required for certain businesses are defined.

It is through the analysis of external factors that it is possible to obtain information on the progress of the organization, as well as receiving the feedback from the external environment that is necessary to know if what is being done is really meeting the existing demand in an efficient manner. In addition, changes directly influence the organization, so that it is always prepared to undergo changes that will improve the organization in which it operates.

2.1.5 People Management Policies and Processes

The fact that an organization is based on people shows just how important the people management area is within it, as these are the people who sell, produce, define and set targets in line with the organization's finances. According to Costa (2016), today's great challenge is to manage human resources well, because it is human resources that obtain and maintain competitive advantages. It is necessary to know how to select appropriately and correctly, develop the capabilities of leaders, know how to serve customers, reward good performance, control costs and maintain fair treatment of employees.

According to Costa (2016) "the people management process involves: Provision Process, Application Process, Maintenance Process, Development Process and Monitoring Process."

- Provisioning process: this is inserted in the context of planning and recruiting people who are qualified and meet the needs required to carry out the job in the specific position. The recruitment of these people can be either internal, where someone who already works within the organization does the recruitment, or external, where it expands to the external recruitment environment (COSTA, 2016).

- Application Process: encompasses the design and analysis of jobs and their performance evaluation. The main objectives of the Performance Appraisal system are: "to provide objective and careful feedback; to identify competencies; to improve communication between people; to obtain relevant information for employee promotion; to bring about changes in company culture; to seek continuous improvement" (COSTA, 2016).

- Maintenance process: this is linked to remuneration and benefits, in which organizations are looking for different forms of remuneration, such as the competency system, since the professional's activity will directly interfere positively with the organization's goals, thus focusing on the person, not the position (COSTA, 2016).

- Development process: people are trained, showing them what they know, because knowledge must be disseminated, so that people learn how to carry out their jobs in the best possible way, as well as being prepared for the frequent changes that can always happen (COSTA, 2016).

- Monitoring process: is characterized by stimulating the self-control and flexibility that the professionals who are present in the organization, to have attitudes of cooperation and seek the effective achievement of its mission. With this, the organization must be prepared to control and really see if the employee who is exercising that function is definitely the most appropriate for the job (COSTA, 2016).

With this, the need for self-fulfillment of employees is again affirmed, so that when they are selected, they participate in decision-making, and carry out their function in a motivating and satisfying way, feeling like a collaborator within the organization in which they are inserted (COSTA, 2016).

2.2 PEOPLE MANAGEMENT

Companies that want to survive in today's market need to be constantly adapting to market conditions and changes. They need to revise their production processes in order to produce better quality products at lower costs, seeking to innovate at all times, creating products in line with customer expectations and, to do this, it is essential to pay attention to people (COSTA, 2016).

When you think about people management, you can't think that this reality has always existed, nor have people always been thought of as the main asset of an organization. Human relations are a process of integration with other individuals in a work situation, so that workers collaborate with the organization and find satisfaction for their social and psychological needs (GIL, 2007, p. 19).

The fact that an organization is based on people shows how important the area of people management is, being in various areas such as sales, production, defining designers, as well as setting targets for all sectors of the organization. According to Costa (2016), on the Administradores website, today's great challenge is to manage human resources well, because it is human resources that obtain and maintain competitive advantages. It is necessary to know how to select properly and correctly, develop leadership profiles, know how to serve customers, reward good performance, control costs and maintain fair treatment of employees (ALBUQUERQUE *et al.*, 2009).

People management is characterized as "a set of policies and practices that allow the reconciliation of expectations between the organization and the people so that both can achieve them over time" (DUTRA, 2002, p.17). In this definition, we can see two main points. The first, which states that people management is a set of policies and practices, and the second, which mentions the reconciliation of expectations between the organization and people.

According to Barbieri (2012, p.3): "Companies are fighting for results and for a future full of success. This struggle is not just about market share, but also about intellectual leadership". For Chiavenato (2010), people management is made up of people and organizations, where people spend a large part of their lives working within organizations and depend on them to function and achieve success.

"People management is now playing a leading role in achieving the organizational excellence needed to face competitive challenges such as globalization, the use of new technologies and the management of intellectual capital" (GIL, 2007, p. 60).

The professionals who work in the People Management area are also known as those responsible for HR. This area is made up of various subsystems, but few company directors, or even the professionals themselves, understand the importance and complexity of this field. In view of this, it can be said that in a systematic way, Human Resources management has gone through difficulties in order to be as it is today. It has faced various challenges in order to really show its need and importance within organizations, until it understood that the employee is like a partner, since the production process depends on a joint action, where everyone seeks greater satisfaction and the achievement of their objectives (REIS, 2005).

2.2.1 Knowledge

Knowledge is said when we can make an association between the individual and their practical experience, when the information can be understood by another individual. To say that you know something about a city, for example, not just by reading newspapers or magazines, but by actually having been there, then you really know it. Matos (2003) defends what Luckesi (1996) says about knowledge, defining it as:

> "The explanation/elucidation of reality stems from an investigative effort to discover what is hidden, what is not yet understood. Only once an object has been understood in its way of being can it be considered known. Acquiring knowledge is not understanding reality by retaining information, but by using it to unveil the new and move forward, because the more competent the understanding of the world, the more satisfactory will be the action of the subject who possesses it" (MATOS, 2003, p.1).

According to Drucker (2002, p.32), "knowledge today is considered to be proven through action. What this means today is that knowledge is information that becomes action and is focused on results. These results are seen outside the person, in society and the economy, or in the progress of knowledge itself." Knowledge is an increasingly important asset for a company, because it is through knowledge that its employees enable the company to innovate and produce higher quality products. Companies therefore need to provide support that allows knowledge to be shared between company members, through meetings, training, workshops, teleconferencing and other means of communication.

Spender (1996, p.67, *apud* LOIOLA; NERIS; BASTOS, 2006, p. 120) defines tacit knowledge as "knowledge that has not yet been abstracted from practice". This is knowledge that individuals have acquired throughout their lives, through their experiences. Explicit knowledge, unlike tacit knowledge, can be easily transmitted within the organization and does not require personal contact to be shared.

The knowledge of human resources makes all the difference within an organization, as they will be the mentors when a new employee joins the team. Those who have the most experience of the organization's business have the highest levels of leadership and management, because they have the knowledge and are able to guide the progress of the activities carried out by the teams or work groups.

2.2.2 Competency Management

The authors Kilimnik and Sant'Anna (2006) note that the concept of competence is neither new nor recent. It is a considerably old idea that has been revived in the present day due to the many changes that have impacted on the world of work, such as the ongoing processes of productive restructuring, the unpredictable environment in the economy, transformations in organizational management models and the phenomenon of globalization. "These aspects have required organizations to have a broad adaptive capacity, as well as a systematic search for elements aimed at ensuring sustainable competitiveness" (KILIMNIK; SANT'ANNA, 2006, p. 90).

According to Resende (2003, p. 30), there are numerous meanings for the word competence. The term has been used, more traditionally and frequently, with the following meanings:

Incumbency: "This is your responsibility".

Suitability: "The person appointed is competent to take charge of the group".

Decision-making power: "Only the board of directors has the power to resolve this issue."

Sufficiency: "He is competent enough to handle the matter."

Dutra (2001, p. 25-26) explains that the concept of competence has become part of the world of organizations, more specifically in the area of people management, due to the intense transformations experienced in the world of work which, according to him, have had consequences for the way people are managed within companies. For the authors Carbone, Brandao, Leite and Vilhena (2006), individual, personal or human competencies are understood as synergistic combinations of knowledge, skills and attitudes, expressed through professional performance in a given organizational context, adding value to people and organizations.

The author Resende (2003, p. 59) lists the following categories of competencies:

Intellectual skills: (the application of mental abilities);

Cognitive*:* (intellectual capacity with mastery of knowledge);

Relational*:* (involves practical relationship skills and interactions);

Social and political*:* (participation in society);

Didactic-pedagogical: (focused on education and teaching). Methodological*:* (application of techniques and means of organizing activities and work);

Leadership*:* (personal skills and knowledge of techniques).

Although Rogerio Leme (2012) states that all competencies, whether technical or behavioral, are made up of the CHA, since a competency is the set of these elements (knowledge, skills and attitudes), in order to present the definition of technical and behavioral competencies, the author didactically separated the CHA into these two groups of competencies.

• **Technical skills:** everything a professional needs to perform their role. They are expressed by the C and H of CHA, i.e. Knowing and Knowing How.

• **Behavioral competencies**: this is the competitive edge of each professional and has an impact on their results. It is expressed by the A of CHA, i.e. the Want to Do.

According to Souza (2011, p.91), this is a combination of approaches with the same objectives and which complement each other in a very productive way, where "Competency Management lends a qualitative structure necessary for the work of leaders, who as coaches make use of these facilities to implement their management process". It is currently one of the most powerful tools for giving meaning to employees (leaders or future leaders), committing them to their own results in line with those of the organization.

2.2.3 Human Resources in Projects

Human resource management in projects includes some processes that better organize and manage the project team as a whole. The team that is part of the project should have designated roles and responsibilities until the project is completed, bearing in mind that the type and number of project team members may change frequently throughout the project (PMBOK, 2008, p.181).

The human resources sector is responsible for creating an organizational infrastructure through excellence in the services offered and efficiency in administrative processes. With the role of people manager, it is the HR department's responsibility to encourage employee contribution, commitment and training when necessary.

The project management team is a subset of the project team and is responsible for project management activities, involving leadership in initiating, planning, executing, monitoring, controlling and closing the project phases. According to the PMBOK (2008, p.181), roles and responsibilities specify which members of the project team should be assigned, as the involvement of all team members in project planning and decision-making can be beneficial.

Within human resource management there are the following processes (REIS, 2005):

- Developing the human resources plan: this process involves documenting the roles, responsibilities and skills required in relation to the project hierarchy, as well as creating a personnel management plan.
- Mobilizing the project team: this process verifies that human resources are available.
- Developing the project team: a process that improves skills and improves the interaction between the team and the environment.
- Managing the project team: during this process the performance of team members is monitored, providing feedback, resolving issues and managing project changes.

2.2.4 How to motivate human resources

According to Caliper (2007), you need to identify the needs of your employees to avoid wasting time and money. We'll use the example of

Maslow's Pyramid to describe the needs of employees.
collaborators:

Biological and physiological needs: companies must offer fair wages, adequate working hours and rest breaks.

Safety Needs: Organizations need to show employees that they comply with occupational safety regulations, offer life insurance, health and pension plans as benefits.

Social needs: showing employees the need for group work and interpersonal relationships through group projects and lectures.

Esteem needs: recognizing the work and effort of the employee, through praise, promotions, rewards (not necessarily financial).

Self-fulfillment needs: use the ideas of employees, getting them involved in decision-making related to their work, refresher courses and challenging opportunities.

For an employee to be motivated, they need to be performing activities that they enjoy doing, working in harmony with other team members, being paid according to their professional ability, and having benefits to continue providing services to the organization.

Generally what happens in the main organizations is that they only want results and more results and end up forgetting that it is the employees who bring good and bad results to the company, and if the employees are unmotivated they will not bring good results to the organization.

2.2.5 Job analysis and description

The job title means detailing what the job requires of the employee in terms of knowledge, skills and abilities so that they can carry it out properly.

Job analysis is defined with the intention of ensuring the internal consistency of salaries, because each job must be evaluated in terms of the prerequisites for its employees, the effort required and the responsibility that comes with it, including possible errors and the seriousness of their consequences.

- What factors will be considered in the evaluation?
- The number of levels used in these factors.
- The score to be assigned to each level of each factor.

The first stage is the selection of employees for the organization and there are many different techniques, methods and resources for selecting staff. This selection, however, whatever it may be, must start from the basic idea that human beings are the most important factor in all social groups and that each individual has a complex life.

Selection is the recruitment process in which the most suitable person is chosen from among the candidates for the vacancy available in the chosen sector.

The main selection techniques on the market are numerous and can vary according to the type of organization, job title, line of business and, often, the knowledge that the professionals responsible must have to take on the job. But the following are some examples of techniques that can be used:

- Screening: the first contact made with a job candidate.
- Filling in the job application: all the items on this form must be duly completed by the candidates.
- References: obtaining professional references is of great value in understanding the personality traits of candidates.
- Application of tests: these are Portuguese and arithmetic tests, to check that the candidate has the required preparation to carry out the desired job, or another that the selector needs to fill at the time.
- Personality interview: consists of a long interview of thirty, sixty or more minutes if necessary, where the candidate's personality is tested as a decision and choice process where the selection body will decide which of the roughly equivalent candidates will fill the position.
- Simulation: they move away from individual and isolated treatment to

focus on treatment in groups and replace the verbal or execution method with social action. Simulation techniques are essentially group dynamics techniques.

- Group dynamics: group dynamics is part of social psychology and is concerned with the forces at work in the context of a group. Any individual behaves differently when in a group, and a given group varies its behavior depending on the context presented to it.

3 METHODOLOGY

The aim of this work is to describe which roles need to be defined for an IT organization to be able to carry out its activities according to each role and function. In this sense, a case study was carried out to analyze which roles and positions need to exist for a company to be able to develop its products.

In order to describe the importance of this study, a literature review was carried out, explaining each concept addressed and its significance in the study. A search was made for materials already written on the subject to provide a theoretical basis in published articles, which according to Cauchick (2012, p. 54), is "the construction of the objective reality of the research occurs from the perspective of the researcher, based on the literature review and the subjective reality of the individuals captured from multiple sources of evidence in the natural environment of the research".

The case study is used by the researcher in order to answer "how" and "why" questions and is the preferred method for examining contemporary events, where it is not possible to have control over the events (YIN, 2010).

In order to collect the data, we analyzed the job descriptions of the company we studied and found that its old job descriptions did not include the skills and competencies of each professional who worked on projects, making it difficult for professionals to identify what they had already achieved and what they still need to achieve in order to move up the ranks, thus making it easier to improve the company's professionals.

To support this approach, it was possible to have access to the job definitions and profiles of each area of the company studied. For this reason, it is very important for an organization to have a human resources team that is very well aligned and that knows how to classify its assets, which are very precious to it.

4 RESULTS

The results are part of the research as a way of applying theoretical terms into practice. The roles defined within an IT organization are presented below, and these positions and roles were defined from the management of Human Resources teams.

4.1 ROLES AND RESPONSIBILITIES IN THE PROJECT

The human resources plan, as part of the project management plan, provides guidance on which of the project's human resources should be defined, mobilized, managed, controlled and finally released.

• **Role:** describes the part of a project for which a person is responsible and accountable for the results. Examples: civil engineer, business analyst, etc.

Job Mission/Objective: describes the job mission together with the objective of that activity within the software development.

• **Responsibility:** the work that a member of the project team is expected to carry out in order to complete the project's activities.

• **Competence:** the skill and ability needed to complete project activities. If project team members do not have the necessary skills, performance can suffer.

4.1.1 Mapping of projects and responsibilities for each task

Within an organization, roles and functions must be well defined in order for activities to run smoothly. In this sense, the skills that each team member needs to have and according to the activities they will perform within the organization, the human resources team needs to be very careful when selecting the people who will be part of the company.

The following are some possible roles, responsibilities and skills that have been defined within an organization that develops projects related to information technology. For each type of role and function, there are levels such as Trainee, Junior, Full, Senior and Master.

In the position of Trainee, the employee needs to have little knowledge of the area in which he or she will be working, and this is the first step in which the employee is placed in the job plan within any organization.

For an employee who moves up a level to Junior, they need to have all the skills required for the new position and a few more requirements in order to move up a level and get a pay rise, as well as an increase in their obligations according to the level of the position. For an employee who has already entered a level such as Full, they already have greater knowledge and in these cases the salary is higher due to the question of responsibility for the work carried out.

4.1.1.1 Trainee Configuration Analyst

Mission/Purpose of the Position:

Maintain, configure and support integrated tools and environments in order to create environments for software development and/or testing.

The purpose of the position is to apply verification and validation techniques to software development processes and internal testing during the product manufacturing process in order to guarantee product quality in accordance with established plans, procedures and standards.

Main responsibilities:

- Apply standards/guidelines to the change configuration management process.
- Apply and maintain the definitions of the configuration and change management process.
- Evaluate the conformity of the systems' artifact storage structures to the defined process.
- Guide the agencies to ensure that all project-related artifacts are

stored in an integrated manner.

- Apply the definitions of development processes.
- Maintain the configuration management plan (e.g. policies, guidelines, procedures).
- Supporting the organizational areas involved in executing the processes (e.g. monitoring, training and drawing up procedures).
- Participate in closing *baselines* (development timelines) for projects that require configuration and change management.
- Install and configure tools for managing the entire development cycle
- Maintain the configuration management tools used.
- Carry out other related activities and/or those inherent to the procedures of their work process.

Table 1 - Technical Competencies of the Trainee Configuration Analyst

Knowledge and skills	Knowledge of the Office Package
	RTC tool features
	Overview of the main development methodologies/processes
	Relational database concepts
	CMMI/MPS.BR principles
	Tax law
	SCRUM principles
	WSO2 principles
	Development life cycle nodes
	Development life cycle nodes
	Concepts of continuous integration
	Product and service features
	Nopoes in software engineering
	Notes on version control tools
	No tools for continuous integration
	Concepts in configuration management
	Skills in Change Management

	Nopoes in the build process
	Nopoes in computer networks

Source: Prepared by the author

Desirable behavioral skills:

Teamwork, interpersonal relationships, results orientation, flexibility, commitment.

4.1.1.2 Software Quality Assurance Analyst Trainee

Mission/Purpose of the Position:

Apply verification and validation techniques to internal processes and tests during the product manufacturing process, in order to guarantee product quality in accordance with plans, procedures and procedures established standards.

Main responsibilities:

- Create "end-to-end" test pianos for new or updated software products to determine whether the software will perform accurately and reliably according to documented requirements as well as established standards under normal and abnormal conditions.
- Identify test requirements from specifications, map test case requirements and design test coverage plan.
- Maintain effective communication with developers regarding product limitations (e.g. requirements, performance, and/or interface problems).
- Develop, document and maintain functional test cases and other test artifacts, such as test data, data validation, scripts and automated scripts.
- Create and execute test plans and create test reports to describe program evaluation, testing and correction.
- Carry out compatibility tests with external products when necessary.
- Perform manual exploratory and usability tests.
- Complying with company policies, procedures and/or standards, work

processes, internal regulations, confidentiality agreements, quality management systems, the environment, health, safety and labour legislation, as well as ensuring the organization, safety and confidentiality of the documentation, equipment and information under their responsibility, keeping the work environment clean and organized.

- Carry out other related activities and/or those inherent to the procedures of their work process.

Table 2 - Technical Skills of the Software Quality Assurance Analyst Trainee

Knowledge and skills	Knowledge of functional and exploratory testing techniques
	Knowledge of the Office Package
	SOA architecture principles
	RTC tool names
	Nogoes of software engineering disciplines
	Relational database concepts
	BPMN notes
	Creating screen and bank mocks
	General ERP software
	Test strategy dialogues
	Programming logic concepts
	MPS.BR meetings
	SCRUM lessons
	SQL nogoes
	TDD nogoes
	Notes on load testing techniques and tools
	Introduction to performance testing techniques and tools
	Notes on security testing techniques and tools
	Nogoes of the development life cycle
	ERP nogoes in general

Source: Prepared by the author

Desirable behavioral skills:

Teamwork, interpersonal relationships, results orientation, flexibility, commitment.

4.1.1.3 Trainee Developer

Mission/Purpose of the Position:

Develop systems according to the stages and work supports defined in the project schedule, as well as the technical documentation, methodologies, language and tools pre-established, in order to guarantee the quality and full operation of the systems and applications, in accordance with the technical scope of the project and adding value to the client.

Main responsibilities:

- Develop and maintain applications following pre-established standards and methodologies.
- Carrying out unit tests in the development environment, in order to verify that the program is executed correctly, within the specified requirements and meeting the appropriate performance.
- Carrying out white box tests to ensure the basic functioning of what has been developed.
- Complying with company policies, procedures and/or standards, work processes, internal regulations, confidentiality agreements, quality management systems, the environment, health, safety and labour legislation, as well as ensuring the organization, safety and confidentiality of the documentation, equipment and information under their responsibility, keeping the work environment clean and organized.
- Carry out other related activities and/or those inherent to the procedures of their work process.

Table 3 - Technical Competencies of the Developing Trainee

Knowledge and skills	Knowledge of the Office Package
	SOA architecture principles
	RTC tool names
	Nogoes of software engineering disciplines
	General ERP software
	MPS.BR meetings
	Object-oriented programming concepts
	SCRUM lessons
	SQL nogoes
	TDD nogoes
	Nogoes of the development life cycle
	ERP names
	Nogoes in software engineering
	Programming language notes

Source: Prepared by the author

Desirable behavioral skills:

Teamwork, interpersonal relationships, results orientation, flexibility, commitment.

4.1.1.4 Junior Business Analyst

Mission/Purpose of the Position:

Monitor and analyze the life cycle of products in order to ensure technical positioning and competitiveness in the market, meet customer needs, achieve and/or exceed pre-established sales targets and margins, and increase market share.

Main responsibilities:

- Participate in the product roadmap in order to evaluate changes to products and/or new languages in relation to market trends and customer needs.
- Participating with the EPG (Process Engineering Group) in analyzing and deciding on investments in improvements or new

products.

- Accompanying the product during the manufacturing phases in order to provide technical support, as well as carrying out the necessary interfaces with the client.
- Carrying out approvals of requirements during the internal process, playing the role of the external client, as well as accepting the product and/or involving the client according to the characteristics or strategy of the application.
- Support the P.O *(product owner)* during the product development phases.
- Coordinating the product approval process.
- Monitoring product performance in the field.
- Maintaining a relationship with the client during the product manufacturing phase.
- Providing support in defining the withdrawal of products from the market with the EPG group (Process Engineering Group), as well as the resulting support with customers (e.g. maintenance, technical support).
- Complying with company policies, procedures and/or standards, work processes, internal regulations, confidentiality agreements, quality management systems, the environment, health, safety and labour legislation, as well as ensuring the organization, safety and confidentiality of the documentation, equipment and information under their responsibility, keeping the work environment clean and organized.
- Carry out other related activities and/or those inherent to the procedures of their work process.

Table 4 - Technical Competencies of the Junior Business Analyst

	Knowledge of the RRC tool
	Knowledge of the RTC tool
	Knowledge of business process management methodology (BPMN notation)
	Knowledge of at least one (1) business area in the building materials and supermarket sectors.
	Knowledge of the organization's development lifecycle
	Knowledge of the product life cycle
	Knowledge of the Office Package
	Knowledge of the company's products and services and their application in the customer process
	SOA architecture principles
	Project management courses (PMI and agile)
	Project management lessons with PMBOK
	SCRUM lessons

Source: Prepared by the author

Desirable behavioral skills:

Teamwork, interpersonal relationships, results orientation, flexibility, commitment.

4.1.1.5 Junior Quality Analyst

Mission/Purpose of the Position:

Carrying out quality assurance activities to ensure that the artifacts produced and the processes used comply with the established plans, procedures and standards.

Main responsibilities:

- Supporting process audits in order to verify the project's adherence to the defined standards and processes.
- Record and follow up, together with project management, on corrective actions relating to identified non-conformities and opportunities for improvement to be implemented within the project.
- Ensuring support to deal with non-conformities.
- Supporting the consolidation of information related to quality assurance within the project, in order to report on the activities carried out.
- Collecting, reporting and analyzing metrics related to the quality assurance process, as well as taking support resulting from the analysis carried out.
- Complying with company policies, procedures and/or standards, work processes, internal regulations, confidentiality agreements, quality management systems, the environment, health, safety and labour legislation, as well as ensuring the organization, safety and confidentiality of the documentation, equipment and information under their responsibility, keeping the work environment clean and organized.
- Carry out other related activities and/or those inherent to the procedures of their work process.

Chart 5 - Technical skills of the Trainee Quality Analyst

Knowledge and skills	Knowledge of the RTC tool
	Knowledge of writing techniques and the preparation of formal texts
	Knowledge of the Office Package
	Notes on formal project management practices (PMBOK)
	Notes on software engineering practices, including agile practices
	CMMI/MPS.BR courses
	SCRUM lessons
	Programming language notes

Source: Prepared by the author

Desirable behavioral skills:

Teamwork, interpersonal relationships, results orientation, flexibility, commitment.

4.1.1.6 Database Architect Trainee

Mission/Purpose of the Position:

Maintaining the architecture and managing the data of the software ecosystem in order to meet the demands of the data applications and maintain data integrity.

Main responsibilities:

- Support programmers and developers in building and optimizing queries (language for extracting reports) used by applications.
- Validate the queries (language for extracting reports) developed for the applications, in order to guarantee their consistency, standards and performance.
- Identify the source of data inconsistencies caused by application or database objects.
- Select resources and systems to meet business information needs
- Complying with company policies, procedures and/or standards, work processes, internal regulations, confidentiality agreements, quality management systems, the environment, health, safety and labour legislation, as well as ensuring the organization, safety and confidentiality of the documentation, equipment and information under their responsibility, keeping the work environment clean and organized.
- Carry out other related activities and/or those inherent to the procedures of their work process.

Table 6 - Technical Competencies of the Trainee Database Architect

Knowledge and skills	Knowledge of the RTC tool
	Programming language notes

	Scope of formal project management practices (PMBOK)
	CMMI/MPS.BR principles
	SCRUM principles
	Concepts of software engineering practices, including agile practices.
	Knowledge of the Office Package
	Knowledge of writing techniques and the preparation of formal texts

Source: Prepared by the author

Desirable behavioral skills:

Teamwork, interpersonal relationships, results orientation, flexibility, commitment.

4.1.1.7 Project Leader

Mission/Purpose of the Position:

Supporting the project management team in the construction of the project, providing technical guidance to the team and carrying out technical activities, if necessary, in order to achieve the project's objectives and expected results.

Main responsibilities:

- Support the project management team in the management of resources made available by the pool in their respective projects, as well as in the management of the project to which it is allocated.
- Supporting the project management team in the management and execution of the individual training plan for their project resources.
- Provide the technical leveling of your project's human resources, striving for excellence in the activities carried out.
- Carry out technical activities within the project if necessary.
- Guide the project management team in the use of defined techniques, standards, policies and guidelines.
- Be co-responsible for meeting the project's goals and objectives.

- Promote the integration and cohesion of your project collaborators.
- Be co-responsible for the management and execution of projects following the process determined by the PMO.
- Ensuring adherence in the management and execution of projects to the processes described and published by the EPG (Process Engineering Group).
- Contribute to the EPG (Process Engineering Group) for the evolution and maintenance of the defined processes.
- Contribute to creating an environment that fosters unity and values teamwork.
- Support the project management team by providing feedback on technical aspects to each member of the project team.
- Resolving impediments reported by the team in order to protect the project's objectives and goals.
- Technically leading teams, planning and monitoring the progress of activities and providing all the necessary technical support in order to achieve and/or exceed business objectives.
- Comply with company policies, procedures and/or standards, work processes, internal regulations, confidentiality agreements, quality management systems, the environment, health, safety and labor legislation, as well as ensuring the organization, security and confidentiality of documentation, equipment and information under their responsibility.
- Carry out other related activities and/or those inherent to the procedures of their work process.

Chart 7 - Technical Competencies of the Project Leader

Knowledge and skills	Knowledge of project management techniques
	Knowledge of conflict resolution techniques
	Knowledge of leadership and people management techniques
	Knowledge of the Office Package

	Knowledge of cloud computing
	ERP knowledge
	Knowledge of agile testing techniques
	Mastery of software engineering
	Mastery of project management tools
	Mastery of the RTC tool
	Mastering the development lifecycle
	Mastery of SCRUM

Source: Prepared by the author

Desirable behavioral skills:

Teamwork, interpersonal relationships, results orientation, flexibility, commitment.

4.1.1.8 ERP Service Analyst

Mission/Purpose of the Position:

Providing remote or face-to-face technical support to users of the company's systems (e.g. clarifying doubts, testing system functionalities, opening technical tickets), in order to meet customer needs and strive for excellence in the services provided. In general, this role/function deals with and solves problems of low, medium and high complexity.

Main responsibilities:

- Providing service via remote connection tools (e.g. telephone, chat, e-mails) or in person at the customer's premises.
- Identifying, understanding, seeking further information, analyzing and solving problems relating to technical calls in order to provide excellent customer service.
- Opening technical tickets, monitoring the resolution of problems and closing tickets using the tools available.
- Present risk situations to their superior based on an assessment of the technical calls handled.
- Supporting the management of action plans resulting from technical

calls, in order to guarantee the software's operational and usability conditions.

- Providing remote or face-to-face training to customers and internal employees.
- Create and execute database commands.
- Act as leader of the service cell when assigned.
- Complying with company policies, procedures and/or standards, work processes, internal regulations, confidentiality agreements, quality management systems, the environment, health, safety and labour legislation, as well as ensuring the organization, safety and confidentiality of documentation, equipment and information under their responsibility, keeping the work environment clean and organized.
- Carry out other related activities and/or those inherent to the procedures of their work process.

Chart 8 - Technical Skills of the Full ERP Service Analyst

Knowledge and skills	Knowledge of project management techniques
	Knowledge of remote and face-to-face service techniques
	Knowledge of training techniques
	Knowledge of the Office Package
	Mastery of the Windows operating system

Source: Prepared by the author

Desirable behavioral skills:

Teamwork, interpersonal relationships, results orientation, flexibility, commitment.

4.1.1.9 Commercial Manager

Mission/Purpose of the Position:

Carrying out the administrative sales process, in order to ensure that closed orders are released, authorized and sent for invoicing in accordance with commercial policy.

Main responsibilities:

- Receiving and analyzing sales orders in relation to the data needed to process sales (e.g. registration data, type of sale, commercial conditions).
- Validate orders and issue the order for invoicing.
- Analyze and check the commission of those involved in sales orders and inform the Finance department.
- Receive, analyze and carry out the relevant administrative process regarding customer support in relation to the original contract (e.g. module and access replacement, service change, registration change, contract cancellation).
- Complying with company policies, procedures and/or standards, work processes, internal regulations, confidentiality agreements, quality management systems, the environment, health, safety and labour legislation, as well as ensuring the organization, safety and confidentiality of the documentation, equipment and information under their responsibility, keeping the work environment clean and organized;
- Carry out other related activities and/or those inherent to the procedures of their work process.

Chart 9 - Technical skills of the Commercial Manager

Knowledge and skills	Knowledge of commissioning policies and tables
	Overview of the product and service portfolio and application in the customer process
	Knowledge of the Office Package

Source: Prepared by the author

Desirable behavioral skills:

Teamwork, interpersonal relationships, results orientation, flexibility, commitment.

4.1.1.10 Seller

Mission/Purpose of the Position:

Carrying out the relationship process with the customer portfolio, promoting and generating new business opportunities for new products and services, in order to get closer to and build customer loyalty and consequently meet the sales targets set by the company.

Main responsibilities:

- - Visiting clients and *prospects,* according to a pre-established schedule or via the PAP (door-to-door) system, to demonstrate the company's products and services.
- Gather all the necessary information on the opportunities identified (e.g. product, solution, services, client profile, application), in order to help prepare the technical and commercial proposal.
- Issuing commercial proposals and conducting the negotiation process with the client in order to close the deal.
- Making telephone contacts, visits, revisits and negotiating the values of active commercial proposals and those with no feedback from the client.
- Keep records of telephone contacts, visits, revisits and negotiations in the commercial management tool.
- Participate in fairs and events, as assigned by the immediate superior.
- Provide sales forecasts, sales results and competitor support to your immediate superior.
- Attend meetings to present monthly, quarterly and annual results.
- Order and keep up-to-date support materials (e.g. folders, giveaways, demonstration DVDs).
- Requesting travel advances for the purchase of bus tickets, airline tickets, car rental or other expenses, as well as rendering accounts.
- Monitoring the implementation of products and services sold.
- Marketing products and accesses added to the system;
- Marketing services added to products;
- Negotiate critical situations related to support and sales, involving technical hours, regardless of whether they will be charged, but with the aim of

resolving the situation amicably with the customer. This may lead to a visit from an analyst and/or remote service.

- Resolve critical situations related to calls that are in the Budget Submission phase;
- Open tickets for all products and services that have been sold to be forwarded to schedule the service to be carried out. When it comes to open hours, the call will be forwarded for invoicing once the work has been completed;
- Promoting the new products and services to be marketed to customers in the portfolio;
- Providing commercial clarification and helping customers to solve problems in relation to service reports in order to meet their needs. If technical clarification is required, the Analyst should be involved in the conversation with the Client;
- Negotiating prices and deadlines with clients, using customer service reports, within the limits set by the company;
- Complying with company policies, procedures and/or standards, work processes, internal regulations, confidentiality agreements, quality management systems, the environment, health, safety and labour legislation, as well as ensuring the organization, safety and confidentiality of the documentation, equipment and information under their responsibility, keeping the work environment clean and organized.
- Carry out other related activities and/or those inherent to the procedures of their work process.

Chart 10 - Salesperson's technical skills

Knowledge and skills	Knowledge of clients' business areas
	Knowledge of the company's standards, procedures, rules and commercial policies
	Knowledge of the Office Package
	Knowledge of conflict resolution techniques

	Knowledge of public speaking techniques
	Knowledge of ERP software
	Mastering trading techniques
	Existing technologies and constraints
	Mastery of the product and service portfolio and its application in the customer process.

Source: Prepared by the author

Desirable behavioral skills:

Teamwork, interpersonal relationships, results orientation, flexibility, commitment.

5 CONCLUSION

The aim of this work was to describe what roles and positions are necessary for an IT organization to be able to work with certain types of roles in its teams. In this sense, once the human resources team standardizes what each person does and is within an organization, it becomes much easier to manage all aspects of the employee's personal and professional growth.

It's much easier for managers to define the activities for each employee, knowing what their role is and what activities they can actually do, because their profile has been properly defined within the company. That's why it's so difficult and important for these roles to be well defined.

One of the advantages of this definition is when it comes to evaluating employee performance, because this is how it is possible to check whether they are achieving their goals and whether they need some kind of recognition for achieving them. When it comes to evaluating their team members, it's much easier for leaders because they've already defined what skills each employee needs to have in order to earn some kind of benefit from the company.

This article has achieved its objective, which was to define each profile and position for employees in IT-related institutions. And here's a tip for companies that want to define competencies and responsibilities regardless of which market area they are targeting. It's much easier to work when these profiles are well defined, as leaders will have more autonomy when it comes to leading and delegating activities to the right people.

Many companies can adopt this practice to better organize their software development teams, acquiring people who are more qualified for the role in which they are working, a better way of organizing resources into roles and positions. And for HR, it's much easier to control the hiring and training needs of employees. Future studies could analyze the definition of roles and profiles in companies other than the IT sector.

REFERENCES

ALBUQUERQUE, Lindolfo Galvao de; LEITE, Nildes Pitombo. Strategic people management: concept, evolution and vision. In: ALBUQUERQUE, Lindolfo Galvao de; LEITE, Nildes Pitombo (Org.). **Gestao** de **pessoas: perspectivas estrategicas**. Sao Paulo: Atlas, 2009.

BARBIERI, Jose Carlos; REIS, Jorge Emanuel. **Corporate social responsibility and sustainable business: from theory to practice.** 2ª ed. Sao Paulo: Saraiva, 2012.

CARBONE, P. P.; BRANDAO, H. P.; LEITE, J. B. D.; VILHENA, R. M. P. **Gestao por Competencias e gestao do conhecimento**. Rio de Janeiro: Editora FGV, 2006.

CHIAVENATO, Idalberto. **Human Resources. The Human Capital of Organizations**. 8th ed. Sao Paulo, Atla, 2008.

Idalberto. **People management: the new role of human resources in organizations.** 3. ed. Rio de Janeiro: Elsevier, 2010.

Idalberto. **Building talent.** Rio de Janeiro: Elsevier, 2012.

CAUCHICK, Paulo Augusto. **Research methodology for production engineering and operations management** [electronic resource] / Miguel (organizer). - Rio de Janeiro: Elsevier: ABEPRO, 2012.

CALIPER. How to motivate Greeks and Trojans? Available at:< http:llcaliper.com.br/sistema-de-avaliacao-de-desempenho>. Accessed on: March 30, 2016.

COSTA, Carlos Eduardo. **People management processes.** Available at: < http:llwww.administradores.com.br/producao-academicalos-processos- de-gesao-de-pessoasl519>. Accessed on: February 26, 2016.

DRUCKER, Peter F. **The best of Peter Drucker: Man, Management, Society.** Sao Paulo: Nobel, 2002.

DUTRA, **Gestao por competencias: um modelo avangado para o gerenciamento de pessoas**. Sao Paulo: Editora Gente, 2001.

., J.S. **Gestao de Pessoas: Modelo, Processos, Tendencies e**

Perspectives. Sao Paulo: Atlas: 2002.

GIL, Antonio Carlos. **People Management.** Focus on Professional Roles. 1ª ed. Sao Paulo, Atlas, 2007.

FISCHER, A.L. A **conceptual and historical review of people management models. In: People in the organization**. Sao Paulo: Gente, 2000.

FLEURY, Maria Tereza Leme (Coord.). **As pessoas na organizapao**. Sao Paulo: Gente, 2002.

KILIMNIK, Z. M.; SANT'ANNA, A. S. **Organizational modernity, people management policies and professional competencies.** In: BORGES-ANDRADE, J. E.; ABBAD, G. S.; MOURAO, L. Treinamento, desenvolvimento e educapao em organizapoes e trabalho: fundamentos para a gestão de pessoas. Porto Alegre: Artmed, 2006, p. 85-96.

LACOMBE, F.; HEILBORN, G. **Administrapao: principios e tendencias**. Sao Paulo: Saraiva, 2006.

LEME, R. **Selection and interview by competencies with the behavioral inventory: practical guide to the selection process to reduce subjectivity and efficiency in selection.** Rio de Janeiro: Qualitymark, 2012.

LOIOLA, E.; NERIS, J. S.; BASTOS, A. V. B. **Learning in organizations: mechanisms that articulate individual and collective processes**. In: BORGES-ANDRADE, J. E.; ABBAD, G. S.; MOURAO, L. Treinamento, desenvolvimento e educapao em organizapoes e trabalho: fundamentos para a gestão de pessoas. Porto Alegre: Artmed, 2006, p. 114136.

LUCKESI, C. C. e PASSOS, E.S. **Introdupao a filosofia: aprendendo a pensar**. Sao Paulo: Cortez, 1996.

MATOS, Cleusa Maria Alves de**. Knowledge vs. Information: A necessary discussion.** Espapo Academico magazine, n. 31, Dec. 2003. Available at: <http://www.espacoacademico.com.br/031/31cmatos.htm>. Accessed on February 2, 2016.

PMBOK. **A Guide to Project Management Knowledge.** 4th ed. 2008.

REIS, A. M. V. *et al.* **Team development**. Rio de Janeiro: FGV Ed., 2005.

RESENDE, E. **O livro das competencias: desenvolvimento das competencias: a melhor autoajuda para pessoas, organizapoes e sociedade.** 2. ed. Rio de Janeiro: Qualitymark, 2003.

ROBBINS, Stephen P. **Administrapao: mudanpas e perspectivas**. Sao Paulo: Saraiva, 2000.

SOUZA, P. R. M. **A nova visão do coaching na gestão por competencias: a integrapao da estrategia: como desenvolver competencias na prática, diminuindo subjetividades e ajustando o foco.** Rio de Janeiro: Qualitymark, 2011.

TOMAEL, M. I; ALCARA, A. R.; CHIARA, I. G. **From social networks to innovation**. Ci. Inf., Brasilia, v. 34, n. 2, p. 93-104, May/Aug. 2005.

ULRICH, Dave (org). **Strategic Human Resources**. Sao Paulo: Futura, 2000.

., D. **The champions of human resources: innovating for the best results.** Sao Paulo: Futura, 2003.

WREN. D. A. **The history of management thinking.** Hoboken-NJ: Wiley, 2005.

YIN, Robert K. **Case Study: Planning and Methods**. 4.ed. Porto Alegre: Bookman, 2010.

MIX
Papier aus verantwortungsvollen Quellen
Paper from responsible sources
FSC® C105338

Printed by Books on Demand GmbH, Norderstedt / Germany